Fast Ideas for Busy Teachers

Math

······································

Grade 1

······································

by
Vicky Shiotsu

Illustrations by
Kathryn Marlin

Published by Frank Schaffer Publications
an imprint of

 **Children's Publishing**

Author: Vicky Shiotsu
Editor: Cindy Barden

Children's Publishing

Published by Frank Schaffer Publications
An imprint of McGraw-Hill Children's Publishing
Copyright © 2004 McGraw-Hill Children's Publishing

Send all inquiries to:
McGraw-Hill Children's Publishing
3195 Wilson Drive NW
Grand Rapids, Michigan 49544

Fast Ideas for Busy Teachers: Math—Grade 1
ISBN: 0-7682-2911-1

1 2 3 4 5 6 7 8 9 MAL 07 06 05 04
The *McGraw·Hill* Companies

Table of Contents

© McGraw-Hill Children's Publishing

0-7682-2911-1 *Fast Ideas for Busy Teachers: Math*

0-7682-2911-1 *Fast Ideas for Busy Teachers: Math*

 Introduction

Packed with hundreds of quick tips, fun ideas, and reproducibles, the *Fast Ideas for Busy Teachers: Math* series provides a wonderful resource designed to make a busy teacher's life easier. Ideas for stocking and organizing your math learning center, individual and group activities, games, reproducibles, patterns, puzzles, explorations of concepts, and much more invite students to learn about math through creative and fun hands-on activities.

Fast Ideas for Busy Teachers: Math supplements your math curriculum with warm-up or follow-up exercises, take-home pages, in-class assignments, and rainy-day activities to help students master a variety of mathematical concepts and skills. Organization by content related to various math skills makes it quick and easy to find the material you need, when you need it. A wide variety of open-ended material allows you to adapt activities to meet the specific needs of your class or individual students. Watch enthusiasm for math grow as students discover how valuable and fun learning math can be!

Teacher resource pages include organizational tips, suggestions for manipulatives, patterns, and a variety of individual, partner, and small group activities designed to increase students' understanding of math. Preparation time and supplies needed are minimal and include items normally available in classrooms.

Fast Ideas for Busy Teachers: Math topics and skill areas are based on the current NCTM Principles and Standards for School Mathematics, designed by the National Council of Teachers of Mathematics. They include number and operations; algebra; geometry; measurement; and data analysis and probability skills through problem-solving strategies, reasoning and proof, mathematical connections, representations, and communications. For specific information, see the matrix showing the correlation of the activities and tips to the NCTM Standards.

Fast Ideas for Busy Teachers: Math allows you to plan creative, motivating activities and incorporate them in your math curriculum. Best of all, students' enthusiasm for math grows when math becomes an adventure of fun and discovery!

Meeting the NCTM Standards
◆◆ Correlation Chart ◆◆

	PROBLEM SOLVING	REASONING & PROOF	CONNECTIONS	REPRESENTATION	COMMUNICATION
NUMBER & OPERATIONS	8, 10, 12, 13, 14, 16, 17, 18, 19, 20, 26, 28, 29, 32, 33, 37, 53, 54, 55, 57, 58, 59, 62, 63, 64, 65, 66	7, 8, 9, 14, 26, 27, 28, 29, 30, 31, 37, 55, 57, 59, 60, 62	7, 8, 9, 10, 13, 14, 15, 16, 26, 27, 29, 30, 31, 33, 53, 55, 57, 59, 60, 62, 63, 64, 65, 66	7, 8, 10, 13, 14, 15, 16, 17, 18, 20, 26, 27, 28, 29, 32, 53, 54, 55, 56, 57, 58, 59, 61, 62, 63, 64, 65, 66	9, 10, 17, 19, 27, 33, 53, 63
ALGEBRA	21, 22, 23, 24, 25, 34, 35, 36	23, 34, 35, 36	21, 22, 23, 34	21, 22, 24, 25, 35	34, 35, 36
GEOMETRY	39, 45, 46	39, 42, 43	38, 39, 40, 41, 42, 43, 44	38, 39, 40, 41, 42, 43, 44	38, 39, 42, 43
MEASUREMENT	47, 51, 52, 70, 71, 72, 73, 74, 75, 76, 77, 78	50, 70, 71, 72, 73, 74, 75, 76, 77, 78	47, 48, 49, 70, 71, 73, 75, 76, 77, 78	47, 48, 49, 50, 51, 70, 71, 72, 73, 74, 78	47, 48, 50, 74, 76
DATA ANALYSIS & PROBABILITY	67, 68, 69, 79, 80	79, 80	67, 68, 69, 79, 80	67, 68, 79	67, 68, 69, 78, 79, 80

0-7682-2911-1 *Fast Ideas for Busy Teachers: Math*

Fill the Jars

This estimation activity is a fun way to reinforce students' counting skills. You will need baby food jars and an assortment of counters such as bingo chips, large dried beans, paper clips, buttons, or other items that fit in the jars.

Divide the class into small groups and give each group a jar and set of counters. Challenge students to guess how many counters will fit in their jars. Have the groups record their guesses on the board. Then ask each group to decide on a way to check their guesses.

When they finish, have the groups record their findings beside their estimates.

Some students may count the items as they fill the jar. Others will fill the jar first and count afterwards. Discuss the different methods groups used to find the answer and talk about how there can be more than one "right way" to find the answer.

Keep Manipulatives Organized

A small storage box with many removable drawers provides convenient storage for manipulatives like beads, buttons, game chips, and other small objects.

Fill each drawer with a different type of manipulative. When students need manipulatives, they can take a drawer to their desks. When finished, the student simply returns the drawer to the math center.

Counting Challenge

Write counting questions on index cards and put them in a small paper bag.

Examples:
- How many boys are in class today?
- How many students are wearing red today?
- How many books are on the top shelf?

Each day, ask a different student to draw a card and read the question aloud. Have the class count together to find the answer.

You could also keep a set of counting questions in the math center. Each student visiting the center could draw a card and count to find the answer. Students can write the answers on the back of the cards and return them to the center. They will notice that on different days, the answers to some questions may be different.

 0-7682-2911-1 *Fast Ideas for Busy Teachers: Math*

Counting to 100 and Estimating

Scoop and Count

Divide the class into small groups and give each group a sheet of paper, pencil, and container of counters. Have members of each group take turns scooping as many counters as possible with one hand, counting them, and recording the number. The person in the group who scooped up the most counters is the winner.

For an extra challenge, have students repeat the activity with their other hands to see if they get the same results.

How Many Buttons?

Give each student an index card. Ask students to count the number of buttons on their clothing and draw that number of buttons on their cards. Some students will have several buttons; others may have none. Students should write their names on their cards. Display the cards along the edge of the board or on the windowsill. Have the class count the buttons on the cards to discover how many buttons there are in all.

Count Off

The class can practice counting while playing "Count Off." Decide with the class on a number such as 59 and write it on the board. Then have students take turns counting aloud; the first student says one, the second says two, etc. The child who says 59 wins, and the counting stops.

To vary the game, students can . . .

   Begin with a different number each time
   Count backwards from a starting number
   Skip count

Count Around Your Home

Give each student a copy of the activity, "Count Around Your Home" and ask them to look at the items pictured. Challenge students to estimate how many of each item they think they have at home. After students write down their guesses, they can take their papers home to check their estimates. When students return the papers to school, they can share their results.

Extension:

Have students make a bar graph showing how many they have of each item. Discuss the following questions:

   Which item did you find most often?
   Which item did you find least often?
   What method did you use to make your estimates?

 0-7682-2911-1 *Fast Ideas for Busy Teachers: Math*

Name _____ Date _____

 # Count Around Your Home............................

Look at the items below. How many of each do you have at home?

First, write your guess. Then take your paper home.

Count the items at home to check each guess.

How many windows?

Guess _____

Check _____

How many beds?

Guess _____

Check _____

How many doors?

Guess _____

Check _____

How many tables?

Guess _____

Check _____

How many phones?

Guess _____

Check _____

How many chairs?

Guess _____

Check _____

How many lamps?

Guess _____

Check _____

How many clocks?

Guess _____

Check _____

0-7682-2911-1 *Fast Ideas for Busy Teachers: Math*

Identifying and Ordering Numbers

Checkerboard Math

Laminate a checkerboard. With a permanent marker, write a set of numbers such as 41, 43, 45, and 47 on the red squares of the board. Give students the appropriate number tiles or write the missing numbers on paper circles or game markers. Ask students to place the numbers on the black squares of the checkerboard in the correct order to complete the series. To change the board, remove the numbers with nail polish remover and a paper towel.

Number Line-Up

Cut out 4½" x 6" cards from light-colored construction paper. Write a different number from 1 to 100 on each card. Give each student a card. Call on five or six students at a time to stand in front of the class and ask them to arrange themselves so that their cards appear in order from the least number to the greatest. Repeat the procedure until all students have had a chance to line up in front of the class.

Make Your Own Reusable 100 Number Boards

Hundred number boards are ideal for reinforcing a variety of number concepts. To make sturdy, reusable 100 number boards, make copies of the 100 Number Board on page 11 for each student on cardstock and laminate them so they can be used over and over.

When using the 100 number boards for math activities, students can use dried beans, paper squares, or other small counters to cover the numbers.

Show Me

Give each student a copy of the 100 Number Board (page 11) and a set of counters. Say numbers, one at a time and have students put counters on the corresponding numbers on their 100 number boards.

For variation, use descriptions appropriate to the abilities of your class instead of numbers.

Examples:

Put a counter on the number that comes before/after 18.

Put a counter on the number that is between 34 and 36.

Put a counter on the number that is 10 more/less than 85.

Put a counter on the number that is equal to 3 tens and 6 ones.

Put a counter on the number that equals 7 + 4.

0-7682-2911-1 *Fast Ideas for Busy Teachers: Math*

100 Number Board ....

1	2	3	4	5	6	7	8	9	10
11	12	13	14	15	16	17	18	19	20
21	22	23	24	25	26	27	28	29	30
31	32	33	34	35	36	37	38	39	40
41	42	43	44	45	46	47	48	49	50
51	52	53	54	55	56	57	58	59	60
61	62	63	64	65	66	67	68	69	70
71	72	73	74	75	76	77	78	79	80
81	82	83	84	85	86	87	88	89	90
91	92	93	94	95	96	97	98	99	100

0-7682-2911-1 *Fast Ideas for Busy Teachers: Math*

Identifying and Ordering Numbers

Mystery Letters

Give each student a 100 Number Board (page 11) and 30 counters. Tell students that they will be creating "mystery letters" with their counters. Say numbers one at a time and have students put a counter on each number as you name it. When all of the numbers in the group are covered, they will see the shape of a letter of the alphabet. After they identify the letter, students should remove the counters and start over for the next mystery letter.

Call out these numbers to make the letter F:

| 13 | 14 | 15 | 16 | 17 | 23 | 33 |
| 43 | 44 | 45 | 46 | 53 | 63 | 73 |

Call out these numbers to make the letter J:

| 34 | 35 | 36 | 37 | 38 | 46 | 56 |
| 66 | 76 | 83 | 84 | 85 | 86 | 73 |

Give each student a copy of the activity, "Mystery Letters" to complete individually.

Answers for Mystery Letters: 1. I; 2. H; 3. X; 4. P

Extension:

Let students create their own "Mystery Letters" to share with the class.

Have students form the first letter of their names by placing counters in the appropriate places on a 100 number board.

Mystery Shapes

Students can play "Mystery Shapes" on their 100 number boards. Call out numbers to form geometric shapes such as triangles, squares, and rectangles. Students cover the numbers called with counters, then identify the shapes.

Number Puzzles

Provide each student with a copy of a 100 Number Board (page 11) cut into puzzle pieces. Make each puzzle slightly different. Each piece should have at least six numbers.

Let students put the pieces back together to reconstruct the original number board. After a student completes his puzzle, let him trade with another student. Store puzzle pieces in envelopes or clear zipper-type plastic bags and keep in the math center to use another time.

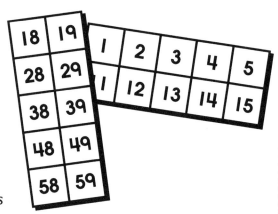

© McGraw-Hill Children's Publishing

0-7682-2911-1 *Fast Ideas for Busy Teachers: Math*

Mystery Letters

Look at each set of numbers.
Cover the numbers on your
100 number board.
Write the letter you made.

1. Cover these numbers.

24 25 26 27 28

36 46 56 66

74 75 76 77 78

What letter did you

make? _____

2. Cover these numbers.

23 27 33 37 43 47

53 54 55 56 57

63 67 73 77 83 87

What letter did you

make? _____

3. Cover these numbers.

13 19 24 28

35 37 46 55 57

64 68 73 79

What letter did you

make? _____

4. Cover these numbers.

14 15 16 17 18

24 28 34 38

44 45 46 47 48

54 64 74 84

What letter did you

make? _____

0-7682-2911-1 *Fast Ideas for Busy Teachers: Math*

Skip Counting and Estimating

Sock Count

Bring in a laundry basket of different-colored, clean, unmatched socks. Ask students to guess how many socks are in the basket and write their estimates on the board. Call on students to find the matching socks and arrange the pairs on a table. Let the class count the socks aloud by 2s to find out how many socks there are in all. Students can compare their estimates with the final total.

Counting Parts of the Body

Let the class use different parts of the body to practice skip counting. Have students hold up their hands and count by 5s or 10s to find out how many fingers are in the room. Record the number on a chart.

Next, students can count by 2s to find out how many feet are in the room. Add that information to the chart. Continue by having students determine how many toes, eyes, and ears are in the room.

Challenge students by asking them to answer other questions:

How many fingers would there be if two more students joined the class?

How many feet would there be if only the girls were counted?

How many hands would there be if two boys left the room?

Skip Counting Manipulatives

Linking cubes and plastic links are ideal for skip counting practice, but other materials are also easy and fun to use. Students can make paper clip chains or attach paper clips to index cards to form sets. They can thread beads or small pasta tubes on pipe cleaners. They could attach clothespins to sheets of cardboard or insert toothpicks into clay bases. Look around to discover many other ideas for skip counting manipulatives.

Dot-to-Dot Number Patterns

Give each student two sheets of white paper. On one sheet, have students use a dark-colored marker to draw a simple picture, such as a house, tree, or fish. Then have students place the blank sheet of paper over their drawings. They should look through the paper to the drawings underneath and draw dots on the top sheet, marking 10 locations along their outlines.

Have students label one dot *Start* and then number the rest of the dots in increments of 2, 5, 10, or other number. Have students exchange papers with a partner and complete each other's dot-to-dot pictures. Then ask students to compare their completed dot-to-dot pictures with the original drawings.

0-7682-2911-1 *Fast Ideas for Busy Teachers: Math*

Skip Counting and Recognizing Number Patterns

Patterns on a 100 Number Board

A 100 number board is a valuable tool for helping students see patterns in skip counting. Give each student a copy of the 100 Number Board (page 11) to use with these activities.

To reinforce counting by tens, have each student place a counter on 10 and on every tenth number after that. Ask students to describe the patterns they see. (For tens, all the numbers end in 0; the number in the tens column increases by one each time.) Repeat the procedure for counting by twos and fives.

Have students place counters on squares to show interesting patterns that develop when counting by threes, nines, and elevens. (Diagonal patterns will appear.) Let students choose one pattern to color on their chart.

Have each student choose a number other than 2, 5, and 10 to skip count by and place counters on the numbers for that pattern. For example, a student who decides to count by fours will place counters on 4, 8, 12, etc. Have students write their number sequence on another sheet of paper.

What Comes in Pairs?

Have students look through magazines and catalogs for things that come in pairs, such as shoes, gloves, earrings, chopsticks, etc. Instruct the class to cut out the pictures and glue them onto a sheet of paper.

Display the pictures on the wall or mount them on a large sheet of art paper. Have students count by twos to determine the number of objects there are altogether.

Count with Casey Caterpillar

Give each student a copy of the activity "Count with Casey Caterpillar." Students choose a number to begin counting from, plus a number to skip count by, and write those numbers at the top of the page. (Example: Begin with 3. Count by 4s.)

Students could use a 100 number board or manipulatives to help determine the numbers in sequence to write on the caterpillar. When they finish, ask students to share any patterns they found. (Example: If starting with 3 and counting by fours, the digits in the numbers end in 3, 7, 1, 5, or 9.)

0-7682-2911-1 *Fast Ideas for Busy Teachers: Math*

Count with Casey Caterpillar.....................

Begin at _____.

Count by _____.

0-7682-2911-1 *Fast Ideas for Busy Teachers: Math*

Adding and Subtracting to 20

Teddy Bear Hunt

Make at least six copies of the "Teddy Bear Cards" on brown paper and cut the cards apart. Before students arrive, hide the teddy bear cards around the room. When they arrive, give each student an envelope and tell them they are going on a teddy bear hunt. Let the class search until they find all the cards.

Let students work in pairs. Ask each pair to add their teddy bear cards together and write the corresponding addition fact on the board. A student with five bears and one who found six bears would write $5 + 6 = 11$.

Students can change partners and write new addition facts. Repeat the activity until they have written a variety of addition facts on the board.

Subtraction Variation:

Make three sets of teddy bear cards on brown paper and three sets on white paper. Repeat the above activity, but have students write subtraction facts instead of addition facts. If two students combined the teddy bear cards they found and had eight brown bears and three white ones, they would write $8 - 3 = 5$.

High Rollers

Divide the class into pairs and give each pair two six-sided dice and a sheet of paper. Instruct each pair to roll the dice, add the two numbers, and record the math fact on their paper. Have students keep a running list of their math facts. Set a time limit and let students see how many addition facts they can roll in one minute or two minutes.

Variations:

Use specialty dice with higher numbers and have students subtract the lesser number from the greater one.

0-7682-2911-1 *Fast Ideas for Busy Teachers: Math*

Teddy Bear Cards...

0-7682-2911-1 *Fast Ideas for Busy Teachers: Math*

Beanbag Math

Make a large 3' x 4' grid on poster board and write a number in each box. Place the grid on the floor and have students stand several feet away. To play, students take turns tossing two beanbags onto the grid.

Players add the two numbers where the beanbags land to get their total score. They write their totals on paper below their names. The student with the highest score wins that round.

Variations:

Make several grids and let students play the game in small groups. Have students play three or more rounds of the game, writing down their scores for each round. At the end of the game, students add up their scores. The player with the highest total wins.

Draw the grid and numbers on the playground with chalk and play outside when the weather is nice.

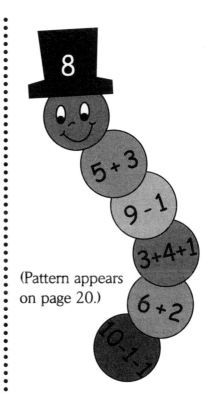

(Pattern appears on page 20.)

Grow, Worm, Grow!

Have students work in pairs. Give each pair a copy of the "Worm's Hat and Body Patterns" on cardstock. They will also need scissors, markers, glue, and construction paper in various colors.

Have students follow these directions:

1. Cut out one circle for the worm's head.
   Use markers to draw the face.
2. Cut out one hat and glue it to the head.
   Write a number on the hat.
3. Cut out at least five more circles.
   On each circle, write an addition or subtraction number sentence that equals the number on the hat.
   Continue gluing the circles together to form the worm's body.
   See how long your worm can grow!

Students could manipulate counters to help find a variety of number sentences.

   0-7682-2911-1 *Fast Ideas for Busy Teachers: Math*

Worm's Hat and Body Patterns................

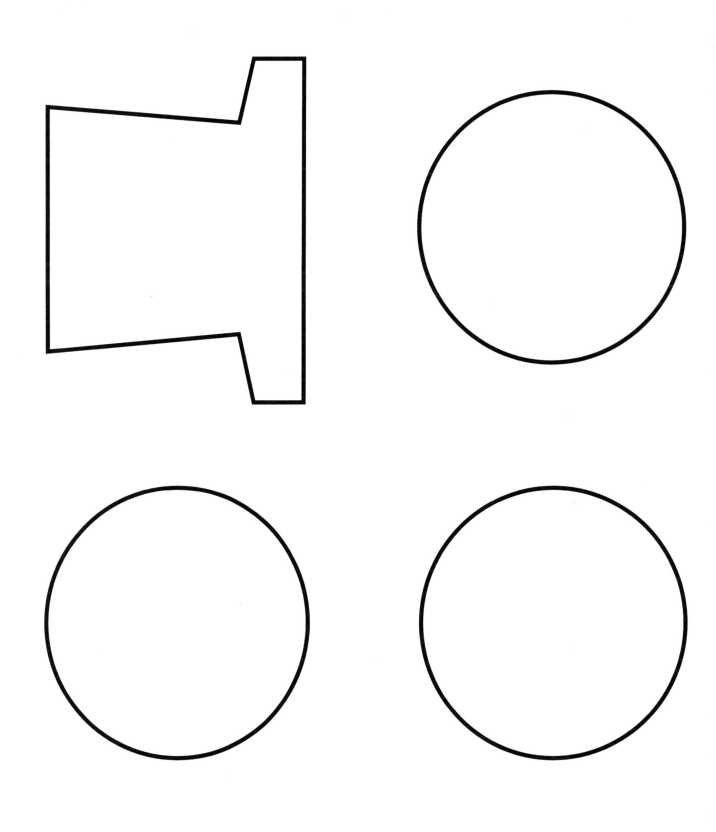

0-7682-2911-1 *Fast Ideas for Busy Teachers: Math*

Fact Families

The Same Number of Stars

Cut five large stars from colored paper. Glue two stars to one page and three stars to another. Hold up the two pages of stars. Together, count the stars on one page, then on the other. Ask how many stars there are in all and have a student write the corresponding equation ($2 + 3 = 5$) on the board. Switch the papers around so they are in opposite hands. Again, count the stars on each page together. Ask another student to write the new equation ($3 + 2 = 5$) on the board. Have the class notice that the sum did not change. Repeat with small manipulatives so that students understand it does not matter in which order numbers are added, the sum remains the same.

Dice Roll

Divide the class into groups of three or four players. Give each group a pair of dice. (The dice could be traditional dice or those with numbers rather than spots.) Have one player in each group roll the dice. The first player in the group to state an addition or subtraction fact related to the numbers rolled earns one point. Have groups continue the game with players taking turns rolling the dice. The first player in each group to score 10 points wins the game.

Jumbo Dominoes Race

In advance, make a set of jumbo dominoes from light-colored construction paper. On the day of the "race," select five students to go to the board. Hold up a domino and tell them to either add or subtract. The students at the board race to see who can write the two corresponding math facts first. The winner of the race stays at the board and four new students enter the race.

If you said "add" while holding up a domino displaying 2 and 5, students would write $2 + 5 = 7$ and $5 + 2 = 7$. If you said "subtract," students would write $7 - 2 = 5$ and $7 - 5 = 2$.

Students not in direct competition participate at their desks using paper and pencils and try to beat the students at the board. Continue until all students have had a chance to go to the board.

As a follow-up activity, students can complete the activity "Domino Math" to create their own dominoes with related addition and subtraction facts.

Domino Math

Fill several zipper-type plastic bags with about 20 dominoes each and place them in the math center. When they have free time, students can choose a bag and use the numbers on the dominoes to write fact families. For a domino with a six and a three, a student would write $6 + 3 = 9$; $3 + 6 = 9$; $9 - 6 = 3$; and $9 - 3 = 6$.

0-7682-2911-1 *Fast Ideas for Busy Teachers: Math*

◆◆ Domino Math ....

Draw dots on the dominoes.

Write number sentences to match the dots.

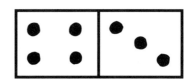

$4 + 3 = 7$
$3 + 4 = 7$
$7 - 4 = 3$
$7 - 3 = 4$

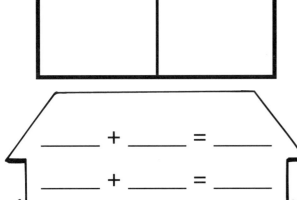

____ + ____ = ____

____ + ____ = ____

____ − ____ = ____

____ − ____ = ____

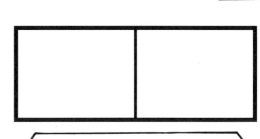

____ + ____ = ____

____ + ____ = ____

____ − ____ = ____

____ − ____ = ____

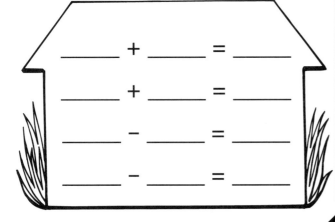

____ + ____ = ____

____ + ____ = ____

____ − ____ = ____

____ − ____ = ____

____ + ____ = ____

____ + ____ = ____

____ − ____ = ____

____ − ____ = ____

0-7682-2911-1 *Fast Ideas for Busy Teachers: Math*

Fact Families

Bean Throw

You will need two-colored dried bean counters for this game. To color the beans, place them on a sheet of newspaper and spray paint them on one side with a bright color.

Divide the class into pairs for the game. Give each pair eight beans and a copy of the activity "Eight Colored Beans." Have partners take turns throwing the beans. Students count the number of beans that landed painted-side up and color the beans on their page accordingly. They then use the bean combinations to write fact families for eight.

If two beans landed with the painted side up, students would write: $2 + 6 = 8$; $6 + 2 = 8$; $8 - 6 = 2$; and $8 - 2 = 6$. Students repeat the activity until they have written six sets of facts on their sheets.

Variation:

Depending on the ability of students, you can increase or decrease the number of beans you give each pair. Use the activity page "Bean Throw Challenge." Draw the appropriate number of beans in each box before copying the page.

Save sets of beans in your math resource center with copies of "Bean Throw Challenge" that include beans drawn for fact families from 10 to 20. Students can use these as rainy-day activities or when they complete their work and have free time.

Chenille Stem(s) and Beads

Using chenille stem(s) and beads of two different colors from the math center, students can explore fact families. Have students thread one to ten beads of one color onto a chenille stem(s), then add another one to ten of a second color. Students use these to write related addition and subtraction facts.

Example: After putting two red beads and four yellow beads on a chenille stem, students would write the following equations: $2 + 4 = 6$; $4 + 2 = 6$; $6 = 4 = 2$; and $6 - 2 = 4$.

State the Facts

For a quick review of related facts, begin by saying, "State the facts for . . . (an addition or subtraction equation, such as $6 + 4$)." Students write the equation and its answer, as well as the other three related facts: $6 + 4 = 10$; $4 + 6 = 10$; $10 - 6 = 4$; and $10 - 4 = 6$. The first student to write all four facts raises his or her hand and, at your signal, stands up and states the family of facts. Repeat the procedure with another pair of numbers.

0-7682-2911-1 *Fast Ideas for Busy Teachers: Math*

◆◆◆ Eight Colored Beans ....

Throw the beans. Color the pictures to show the colors. Write the matching fact families.

5 + 3 = 8
3 + 5 = 8
8 – 5 = 3
8 – 3 = 5

0-7682-2911-1 *Fast Ideas for Busy Teachers: Math*

Bean Throw Challenge.................................

Throw the beans. Color the pictures to show the colors. Write the matching fact families.

5 + 3 = 8
3 + 5 = 8
8 − 5 = 3
8 − 3 = 5

_____   _____

_____   _____

_____   _____

_____   _____

_____   _____

_____   _____

_____   _____

_____   _____

_____   _____

_____   _____

_____   _____

_____   _____

0-7682-2911-1 *Fast Ideas for Busy Teachers: Math*

Place Value to 100

Paper Clip Designs

Give each student 20 to 50 paper clips. Show the class how to link 10 paper clips to form a chain. Then have students make tens and ones with their paper clips and arrange them in an interesting design on a sheet of drawing paper. Tell students that they must keep the groups of tens and ones distinct. Have students write their names on their papers and leave their paper clip designs on their desks.

Give each student a copy of the activity "Paper Clip Designs." They should first write information about their own designs. Then let them walk around the room and look at other designs. Have each student choose five other students' work and determine how many paper clips they used for each design.

Base Ten Buttons

Students need many concrete experiences to develop the concept of place value. Base ten blocks and linking cubes are convenient, but everyday items work well and add variety. You can easily create sets of 10 by gluing 10 beans, macaroni, or small buttons to jumbo craft sticks.

Keep a variety of base ten counters in the math center.

Guess and Score

Divide the class into small groups and give each group a paper plate, 3-inch paper squares (enough for each student to have several), and a container of 50 to 70 small counters. Have one student in each group put some counters on the plate. Group members guess how many counters are on the plate by writing their guesses on the paper squares and placing them facedown.

Next, instruct the group to determine the number of counters by making sets of tens and ones. When they finish, students turn their paper squares faceup. The one with the closest guess collects a counter.

Students continue the activity until everyone in the group has a turn putting counters on the plate. The winner in each group is the one who has earned the most counters.

Clap It

Develop concentration and listening skills with this counting game. Select a digit and write it on the board. Then have the class start counting aloud to 50. Begin at one corner of the room and have each student count off one number. If a student's number has the selected digit in either the ones or the tens place, he claps once instead of saying the number. For an extra challenge, start the count at a higher number, increase the speed, or count backwards.

0-7682-2911-1 *Fast Ideas for Busy Teachers: Math*

Paper Clip Designs ....

Make tens and ones with your paper clips.

Then make a design with your paper clips.

Write about it in the first box on this page.

Look at five other designs. Write how many
paper clips were used in each design.

Ann's design
2 tens and 5 ones
25 paper clips

My design	_____'s design
_____ tens _____ ones _____ paper clips	_____ tens _____ ones _____ paper clips
_____'s design	_____'s design
_____ tens _____ ones _____ paper clips	_____ tens _____ ones _____ paper clips
_____'s design	_____'s design
_____ tens _____ ones _____ paper clips	_____ tens _____ ones _____ paper clips

© McGraw-Hill Children's Publishing

0-7682-2911-1 *Fast Ideas for Busy Teachers: Math*

Place Value to 100 and Estimating

How Many Beans?

Put 30 to 70 beans in each of six small jars and label the jars A through F. Give each student a copy of the activity "How Many Beans?" Students guess how many beans are in each jar. Later, let them check their guesses by calling on students to make sets of tens and ones to find the total number of beans.

Please Pass the Peanuts

Fill a large jar with peanuts in shells. Let the class examine the jar and estimate the number of peanuts. Then pair up students and give every pair a pile of peanuts from the jar. Have each pair separate the peanuts into groups of 10 and bring the leftovers to you. Student volunteers can make sets of 10 with these peanuts and set any leftovers to the side.

As a group, count aloud by tens as you point to each group of 10. Count the remaining ones. One student can write the total number of peanuts that were in the jar on the board. For a special treat, share the peanuts with the class.

Math Book Baskets

Use a large wicker basket, laundry basket, or plastic tote to store featured books with math themes in the math center. Replace the books in the basket periodically to include ones related to the current math unit. Students who complete in-class math assignments early can use their time to select and read a book from the math book basket.

First-grade students usually enjoy the many brightly illustrated books in the *Math Start* series by Stuart J. Murphy as well as the *Math Counts* series by Henry Pluckrose.

Calculator Capers

Have each student work with a partner for this calculator activity. Give each pair a calculator and a container of 50 or more counters. One student should take a handful of counters and arrange them in sets of tens and ones. If the total came to 3 tens and 5 ones, the other student would press the keys 30 + 5 on the calculator. The first student presses the = sign to find the total.

Students switch roles and continue with other numbers.

0-7682-2911-1 *Fast Ideas for Busy Teachers: Math*

How Many Beans? ....

Guess how many beans are in each jar.

Write your guess. Make groups of tens and ones.

Write how many beans there really were.

	My guess	Number of tens and ones	Actual number of beans
A.		_____ tens _____ ones	
B.		_____ tens _____ ones	
C.		_____ tens _____ ones	
D.		_____ tens _____ ones	
E.		_____ tens _____ ones	
F.		_____ tens _____ ones	

© McGraw-Hill Children's Publishing

0-7682-2911-1 *Fast Ideas for Busy Teachers: Math*

Comparing Numbers to 100

Number Construction

Write three digits on the board, such as 2, 3, and 4. Then ask student volunteers to name two-digit numbers using only those digits. Write their responses on the board. (There are nine possibilities: 22, 23, 24, 32, 33, 34, 42, 43, 44.) When all possible two-digit numbers have been listed, have student volunteers circle the greatest number (44) and the least number (22).

Repeat the activity with a new set of numbers. If you choose 0 as one of the digits, there will be only six possible two-digit combinations. For 2, 3, and 0, the possibilities are 20, 22, 23, 30, 32, 33.

Remind students that when they compare numbers with the same number of digits, they should always start with the digit in the highest place value (at the left). The one with the higher number is the greater number. If the digits are the same, students should move to the next digit (to the right) and compare the numbers.

Colorful Number Cards

Students can help make sets of number cards for the math center. Give each student several index cards or 3-inch squares of construction paper. Students can write a number on each card, then use crayons or markers to make the cards colorful and fun. Keep sets of number cards for counting, ordering, and comparing activities.

Number Roll

Make copies of the "Number Dice Patterns." Divide students into pairs and give each pair a copy of the page. They should cut out the patterns, fold on the dotted lines, and tape the sides to make two dice.

Give each pair a copy of the activity "Number Roll." Students take turns rolling their dice. After each roll, students record the two numbers and the greatest and least possible two-digit number they can make with those numbers. After students have recorded six rolls, they determine the greatest and least two-digit number.

0-7682-2911-1 *Fast Ideas for Busy Teachers: Math*

Number Dice Patterns......................

Cut out the patterns.

Fold on the dotted lines.

Tape the sides together to make your dice.

8 | 4 | 6

5

6

7

3

2

1

5 | 4 | 0

© McGraw-Hill Children's Publishing   0-7682-2911-1 *Fast Ideas for Busy Teachers: Math*

◆◆◆ Number Roll..

Work with a partner. Take turns rolling two dice.

1. Write the two numbers you rolled.

2. Write the greatest two-digit number you can make with those numbers.

3. Write the least two-digit number you can make.

	Numbers rolled	Greatest two-digit number	Least two-digit number
Roll 1	_____ _____		
Roll 2	_____ _____		
Roll 3	_____ _____		
Roll 4	_____ _____		
Roll 5	_____ _____		
Roll 6	_____ _____		

What is your greatest two-digit number? _____

What is your least two-digit number? _____

0-7682-2911-1 *Fast Ideas for Busy Teachers: Math*

Place Value Card Game

Make 15 sets of index cards numbered from 0 to 9. (Students could help prepare the cards.) Divide the class into five groups and give each group three sets of cards.

To play the game, players take turns drawing two cards and making the greatest number possible with the digits on the cards. When each player in the group has had a turn, the one with the greatest number wins the round and keeps all the cards from that round.

Play continues until all the cards are gone. The player with the most cards wins the game. If time permits, players can shuffle the cards and play again.

Variation:

Play as above, but have players form the lowest possible number using the two cards they draw. The player with the lowest number in the group wins all cards for that round.

Shake and Roll

Keep a collection of dice in the math center. Include the usual six-sided game cubes with spots, and dice with numbers, ones with more or less than six faces, ones with operation signs, fractions, and larger numbers. Also make extra copies of the "Number Dice Patterns" for students to use for other math games.

Beat My Number

This game is a variation of the card game "War." Cut 2" x 3" cards from cardstock or use index cards. You will need 24 cards for each group of players. Divide the class into groups of two, three, or four players. Give each group a set of cards. Players prepare the cards by writing a random two-digit number on each card.

One player shuffles all the cards and deals them facedown to each player. Players keep their cards in a pile, facedown.

All players in the group turn up their top cards and determine who has the greatest number. That person collects all the cards for the round.

In the event of a tie for the greatest number, the two players with the same number each draw another card. The player with the greater number wins all of the cards played in that round.

If a player loses all of his cards, he is out of the game. The game continues until one player wins all the cards.

0-7682-2911-1 *Fast Ideas for Busy Teachers: Math*

Identifying Patterns

Wagon-Wheel Pasta Patterns

Divide the class into small groups. Give each group a copy of the "Wagon-Wheel Pasta Patterns" page, 50 or more pieces of wagon-wheel pasta, and four 6-inch tagboard squares. Have students study one pattern at a time, then use the pasta to lay out the first three parts of the pattern on three of the squares.

Students should arrange pasta on the fourth square to show what comes next in the pattern, then draw the pattern on the activity page. After they complete the activity, discuss the following questions with the class:

How are patterns A, B, and C the same? (They are "growing" patterns. More pieces are added to each part of the pattern.)

How are patterns A, B, and C different? (Pattern A makes a triangle that grows by one row of pasta each time. Pattern B grows by adding pasta across and then up each time. Pattern C is a square that grows by one row and column each time.)

What helped you figure out what comes next in each pattern?

Follow-Up Activity:

Challenge students to make their own growing patterns using the pasta and tagboard squares. Give them time to experiment by rearranging the pasta in different patterns. When they are satisfied with their patterns, they can glue the pasta to the squares and share their patterns with the class.

Pattern Bookmarks

Small stickers make ideal math manipulatives to help students explore patterns. Give each student or group of students a sheet of stickers. Students can use the stickers to make a pattern on a narrow strip of construction paper to use as bookmarks.

Milk-Jug Cap Patterns

Save colorful, plastic milk- or juice-jug caps for pattern-making activities in the math center. (Ask parents to donate these items, also.)

Store caps with 2½" x 18" strips of drawing paper at the center. Let students glue or tape the caps to the strips to form patterns. Students can arrange the lids to make different kinds of patterns. They could arrange lids by color, alternate between upside down and right side up, or glue them into geometric shapes. Students could also write numbers on the lids to make number patterns.

0-7682-2911-1 *Fast Ideas for Busy Teachers: Math*

Wagon-Wheel Pasta Patterns...................

Look at each pattern.

Use wagon-wheel pasta to make each part of the pattern.

Arrange the pasta to show what comes next.

Draw the answers in the empty boxes.

Pattern A

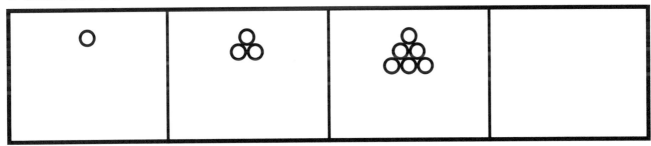

Pattern B

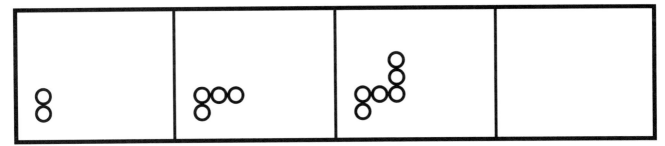

Pattern C

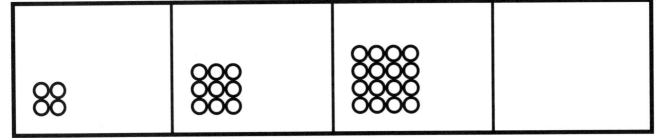

0-7682-2911-1 *Fast Ideas for Busy Teachers: Math*

Identifying Number Patterns and Skip Counting

100 Number Board Patterns

Give each pair of students a copy of the 100 Number Board (page 11) and several small counters. Write a pattern with one missing number on the board.

Example: 1, 3, 5, 7, __, 11, 13.

Tell students to place counters on their boards to mark the pattern. Give them time to discuss the patterns with their partners and suggest possibilities for the missing number. Ask students to share their ideas with the class. Repeat several times with different patterns.

Students can place counters on the 100 number board to make new patterns. Ask one pair at a time to write their pattern on the board and challenge the class to guess the missing number.

Patterns on Display

While working on a unit involving patterns, invite students to bring objects from home that have patterns. Items could include baby quilts, scarves, paper plates, wrapping paper, wallpaper scraps, greeting cards, and other everyday objects.

Help students arrange the items in the math center to create a temporary patterns display.

Skip Count Grid

Give each student a copy of the "Skip Count Grid." Name a number between 0 and 50 and ask students to write that number in the first square at the top left corner of the grid. Tell students to count by ones, two, fives, or tens, to fill in the row. Name a different number for each row of the grid. When correcting the page, you can simply check the far right column to see if a student has counted correctly.

Variations:

Name the first three numbers in each row. Have students write those numbers and continue the pattern by filling in the rest of the boxes in that row. In the far right column, students write the rule that applies, such as + 2 or + 10.

Name three numbers for students to write in the middle of each row. Have them determine the pattern and then instruct them to fill in the beginning and ending numbers for the row.

0-7682-2911-1 *Fast Ideas for Busy Teachers: Math*

Skip Count Grid..

1									
2									
3									
4									
5									
6									
7									
8									
9									
10									

0-7682-2911-1 *Fast Ideas for Busy Teachers: Math*

 # Identifying Geometric Shapes

Shape Booklets

Cut drawing paper in the shapes of large, same-size circles, squares, rectangles, and triangles. Have each student choose a shape and select four matching pages. They should cut back and front cover pages from construction paper in the same shape, then staple the papers between the covers to form booklets.

Have students look through old magazines and cut out pictures of objects with similar shapes. They can glue the pictures onto the pages to complete their shape booklets.

Yummy Shapes

Students can make different geometric shapes using pretzel sticks and/or circle-shaped cereal. Have them glue the shapes onto construction paper for an eye-catching display.

Variation:

Have students use the pretzel sticks and/or cereal to make simple designs by combining several shapes. They can count and record the number of geometric shapes they used in their designs.

Shape Graphs

Make copies of the "Shape Pattern" page on colored construction paper for the math center. Cut out shapes. Fill several envelopes or plastic sandwich bags with about 20 different shape pieces. Include a different number of each shape per envelope with a different total number of shapes in each envelope. Students can count and sort the shapes and make graphs to show how many of each shape are in an envelope.

Shapes on Shapes

Cut geometric shapes from sponges or buy sponge shapes for this math/art activity. Provide each student with a large paper cutout of one of the sponge shapes. Then have students decorate their papers by making colorful sponge prints using tempera paint and the matching sponge. (A student with a large paper triangle would use a triangle-shaped sponge to make prints inside the paper triangle.)

When the paint dries, mount each student's design on a sheet of construction paper. Ask students to write the attributes of their shapes (straight edges, no corners, three sides, etc.) on another sheet of paper. Display the prints and descriptions on a bulletin board to let students share what they learned about their shapes.

 0-7682-2911-1 *Fast Ideas for Busy Teachers: Math*

Identifying Geometric Shapes

String Along

Divide the class into groups of four. Give each group a 12-foot length of string with the ends tied together. Ask students to stand with each member of the group holding part of their "string circles." Give the groups these directions:

Form a circle with the string.

Form a square with the string.

Form a rectangle with the string.

Form a triangle with the string.

Form another triangle different from the last one.

After you finish, discuss the following questions with the class:

Which shape was the hardest to make? Why?

What kinds of things did your group have to think about when you were making the shapes?

Which shapes had the most corners? (square, rectangle)

Which shapes had the most sides? (square, rectangle)

Do you think your group could make a shape that has only two sides?

> **Shapes Wanted**
>
> Ask parents to send extra buttons and plastic lids to school. These objects are great manipulatives for students to use while studying shapes. They are also great for sorting, counting, classifying, and patterning activities.

Shape Hunt

Give each student a copy of the activity "Shape Hunt" to complete. When they finish, students can combine their lists to make a master class list.

Follow up by having students take home a copy of the activity and write the names of four items they find that match each shape.

Build a Shape Creature

Make copies of the "Shape Patterns" on cardstock and cut them out. Students can use the patterns to cut shapes from colored paper or use a ruler and pencil to make their own shapes.

Ask students to arrange their shapes on a sheet of art paper to create interesting creatures and then glue the shapes in place. They can use crayons or markers to add details or cut out "features" from colored paper and attach with glue.

Extension:

During writing class, students could write stories about their creatures and share them with the class.

0-7682-2911-1 *Fast Ideas for Busy Teachers: Math*

Name _____ Date _____

 # Shape Hunt...

Find objects shaped like a circle, square, rectangle, or triangle. List what you found under the matching shape.

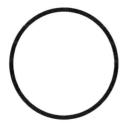   circle

_____
_____
_____
_____

square

_____
_____
_____
_____

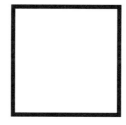   rectangle

_____
_____
_____
_____

   triangle

_____
_____
_____
_____

0-7682-2911-1 *Fast Ideas for Busy Teachers: Math*

Shape Patterns..

0-7682-2911-1 *Fast Ideas for Busy Teachers: Math*

Identifying Solid Figures

Building Fun

Let students work in small groups with wooden shape blocks to build interesting structures. Ask groups to name and describe the shapes of blocks they used. Afterwards, have members of each group count how many they used of each shape and record the information on a chart. Have students look at the chart and find the answers to questions like these:

How many blocks did each group use?

Who used the greatest number of blocks?

Who used the greatest number of cubes? Rectangular prisms? Cones?

Which shape was used most often?

Which shape was used least often?

Shapes Galore

Keep a variety of wooden, plastic, and cardboard geometric shapes such as Ping-Pong™ balls, cylindrical chip containers, toilet paper rolls, facial tissue boxes, oatmeal canisters, small square or rectangular boxes, and film canisters in the math center. Parents are usually willing to donate these types of items. Help students become familiar with the name of each geometric shape and its particular attributes. Give students opportunities to use the shapes for sorting and building activities.

Looking for Solids

Make two copies of the "Solid Figures Patterns" on cardstock. Cut the cards apart. Divide the class into six groups and give each group two cards. (Since pyramids are not common, pair up the pyramid card with one of the more common figures, such as a cube or sphere.)

Have each group take their cards along as they search the classroom, lunchroom, gym, or playground for objects with the shapes pictured on the cards. Students can make a list or draw the objects on paper to show what they found. Let students share their findings with the class.

A Collage of Figures

Have students cut pictures from magazines of objects representing the solid geometric shapes they are studying and use the pictures to make collages. Have students attach an index card to the collage showing a tally of the number of each type of figure in the collage.

0-7682-2911-1 *Fast Ideas for Busy Teachers: Math*

Clay Shapes

Make copies of the "Solid Figure Patterns" page and cut apart the cards. Using the pictures on the cards as models, have students work with clay to form each geometric figure. As students work, ask them to think about the processes they are using to make the shapes. Discuss these questions with the class:

Did you have to roll the clay to form any of the figures?
  If so, which ones?

Did you have to pat down the clay to make it flat in order to form any of the figures?
  If so, which ones?

Which figure was the easiest to make?
  Why?

Which one was the hardest?
  Why?

Trace the Faces

Divide the class into small groups and give each group a collection of cylinders, cones, pyramids, cubes, and rectangles. Have each student choose an object and trace each of its faces on paper.

For a facial tissue box (rectangular prism), students would trace all six faces.

When students finish tracing, have them place their drawings together in one area and the objects they used in another area. Challenge other groups to match drawings with the figures used for tracing.

Helpful Books

Tana Hoban's books are perfect for introducing lines, shapes, and solid figures to the class. *Spirals, Curves, Fanshapes & Lines,* and *Cubes, Cones, Cylinders, and Spheres* are two titles that will delight and captivate students' attention. Read these books to the class to inspire students to make their own photo collection of shapes.

Add these books to the math center so students can study and admire the illustrations over and over.

Another great addition to the math center is *I Spy Schooldays: A Book of Picture Riddles* by Jean Marzollo and Walter Wick. Filled with colorful photographs of shapes and figures, each page presents a picture puzzle using an intriguing arrangement of interesting objects and a rhyme listing the various items to find in the picture.

© McGraw-Hill Children's Publishing 0-7682-2911-1 *Fast Ideas for Busy Teachers: Math*

Solid Figure Patterns

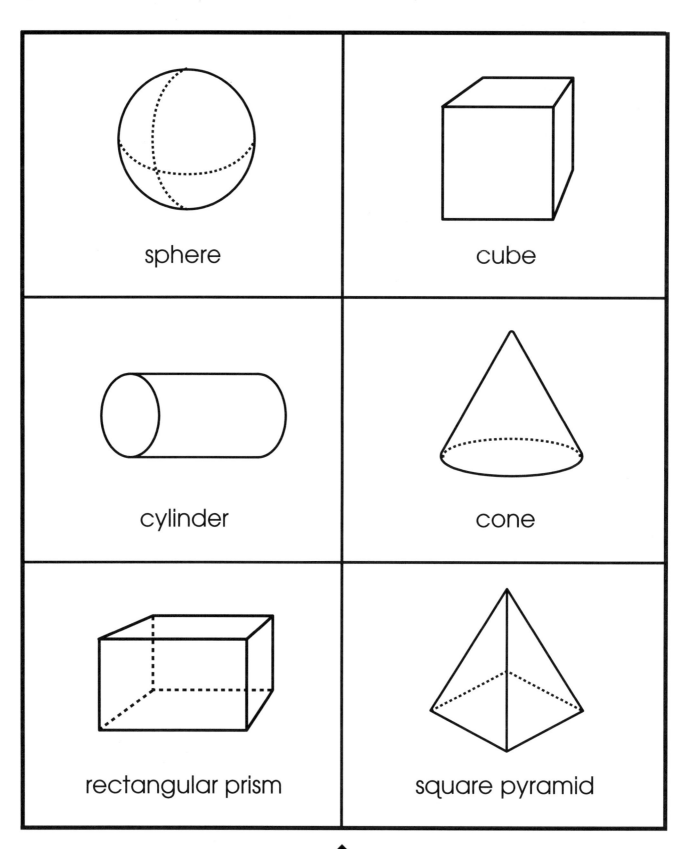

sphere

cube

cylinder

cone

rectangular prism

square pyramid

0-7682-2911-1 *Fast Ideas for Busy Teachers: Math*

# Finding Symmetry

Folded Shapes

Demonstrate making a symmetrical figure by folding a piece of paper in half and drawing half of a heart shape so that the center of the heart runs along the fold line. Cut out the shape and open it. Explain to students that the shape is symmetrical because both halves match exactly.

Then have students fold paper and cut out symmetrical shapes. They do not have to make recognizable shapes. Have students use a marker and ruler to draw a line on the fold line. Explain to students that the line is called a line of symmetry.

Post the shapes on a bulletin board to let the class see the wide variety of symmetrical shapes. Ask students to identify the line of symmetry in each one.

Kite Fun

Give each student a copy of "Kite Fun." Students can decorate their kites with markers to make symmetrical designs and then cut them out. Tape a 12" piece of yarn to the bottom of each kite. Show students how to tie 1½" x 6" strips of crepe paper to the yarn to make a decorative tail. Trim the strips and hang the kites on the wall for a pleasing display.

Symmetrical Bugs

Have students fold colored paper in half. Show them how to draw a simple shape along the fold line. Have students cut out their shapes and open up their papers to see the symmetrical shapes. Then let students make interesting insects from their shapes. Have them add details to symmetrical bugs with markers or crayons. They can cut other features, like legs and antennae from colored paper and glue them on to their bugs. Challenge students to keep their bugs symmetrical. Display the shapes in the classroom for a colorful display.

Mirror, Mirror

Mirrors are a terrific way for students to explore symmetry. Provide small mirrors and a few simple, flat shapes made up of a single, solid color, such as colored paper shapes and plastic cookie cutters. Show students how to hold a mirror perpendicular to a shape. Then have students look at their mirrors to see symmetrical images.

© McGraw-Hill Children's Publishing

0-7682-2911-1 *Fast Ideas for Busy Teachers: Math*

Kite Fun...

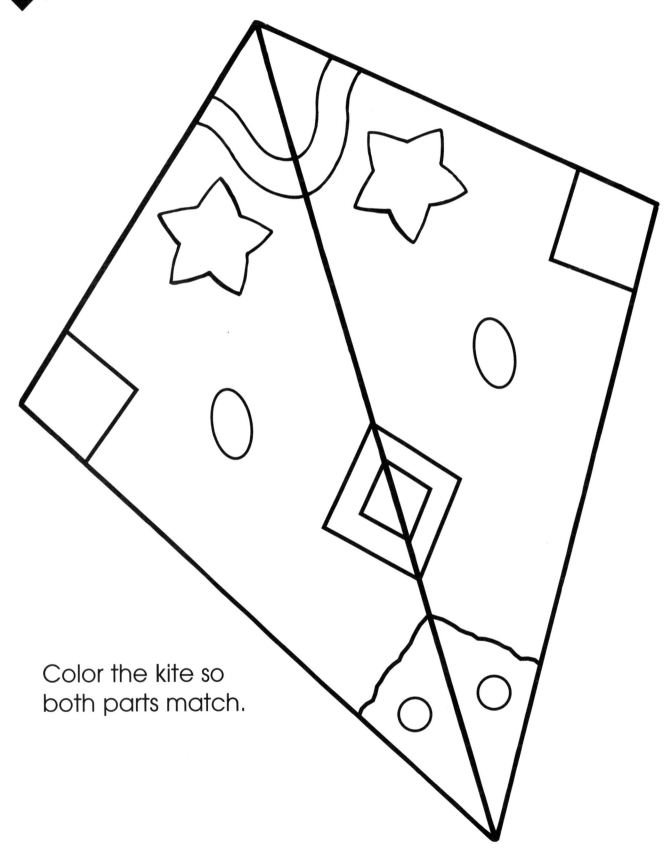

Color the kite so
both parts match.

0-7682-2911-1 *Fast Ideas for Busy Teachers: Math*

Telling Time

Show and Tell

Make a copy of the "Clock Pattern" on cardstock or construction paper for each student. Have students cut out the parts of the clock and assemble them with brad fasteners. Use the clocks with the following activities:

Have students set their clocks for a given time.

Have students show the time and tell what activities they do at that time, such as wake up, leave for school, or watch a favorite TV show.

Say a time. Ask students to show that time on their clocks, then show you and say what time it will be an hour later or an hour earlier.

Tick, Tock, Coffee Lid Clocks

Make durable clock faces with movable hands for the math center using plastic lids from coffee cans or dessert topping containers. Apply twelve peel-and-press dots around the edge and write the numbers 1 through 12 on them. Use a brad fastener to attach tagboard clock hands.

What Did You Do Today?

Talk with students about what they do during the day. They may mention activities such as waking up, eating breakfast, going to school, going to a sports practice, eating dinner, reading a book, watching television, and going to bed. As students mention activities, have them estimate the time when they do each activity.

Divide a piece of chart paper into four sections and label them "morning, about noon, afternoon, and evening." Write the times and activities students suggest in the appropriate sections.

Follow-up by giving each student a copy of "It's Time to . . ." and six sheets of drawing paper. After they complete the activity page, have them cut out the six time strips and glue one strip to each piece of paper. They should draw a picture on each page to match the words, then staple the pages together to make a book.

© McGraw-Hill Children's Publishing

0-7682-2911-1 *Fast Ideas for Busy Teachers: Math*

Clock Pattern

Color the clock.

Cut out the parts of the clock.

Put the clock together.

0-7682-2911-1 *Fast Ideas for Busy Teachers: Math*

It's Time to . . .

Write the time.

Write what you do at that time.

 It's _____ o'clock in the morning. It's time to
_____.

  It's _____ o'clock in the morning. It's time to
_____.

 It's _____ o'clock. It's time to
_____.

 It's _____ o'clock in the afternoon. It's time to
_____.

 It's _____ o'clock in the evening. It's time to
_____.

 It's _____ o'clock in the evening. It's time to
_____.

0-7682-2911-1 *Fast Ideas for Busy Teachers: Math*

Telling Time and Measuring Time

Units of Time

Name several activities and ask students whether it takes closer to one minute or one hour to complete each activity.

Suggestions:

Erase the board (minute)

Count to 100 (minute)

Watch a television program (hour)

Bake a cake (hour)

Wash your hands (minute)

Play a game of soccer (hour)

I Have the Time

Give each student an index card with a time written on it, such as 9:00. Each student's card should show a different time. When the classroom clock matches the time on a student's card, he lets you know by saying, "I have the time!" Give a small treat to students who successfully match the clock with the times on their cards.

Minutes or Hours?

Write two headings on the board: "Minutes" and "Hours." Ask students to brainstorm for activities that take a few minutes or several hours. Write their suggestions under the appropriate headings. For minutes, students may suggest getting dressed, eating lunch, or reading a story. Activities that take several hours might include going to school, driving to another city, and sleeping.

Before or After

Give students practice adding and subtracting hours and half hours. Name a time, such as one hour before 9:30 or one half hour after 10:00. Have students work in pairs to set the appropriate time on their clocks. (They can use the clocks they made with the clock pattern.) One partner can set the hour hand while the other partner sets the minute hand.

Which Hand Is Which?

Use this easy memory trick to help students who confuse the hands on a clock. Cut out an hour hand and a minute hand from tag board and label them with the words minute and hour. Explain that the word "minute" is the longer word and that the minute hand is the longer hand on the clock. The word "hour" is the shorter word and the hour hand is the shorter hand on the clock.

0-7682-2911-1 *Fast Ideas for Busy Teachers: Math*

Adding and Subtracting
Two-Digit Numbers

Place Value Mats

To make a "place value mat" for each student, fold a 12" x 18" sheet of yellow construction paper in half. Glue a 9" x 12" sheet of orange paper to the left half of the paper. Label the orange half "Tens" and the yellow half "Ones." Provide craft sticks or other manipulatives and use the mats with the following activities:

Have students put 23 craft sticks on their mats: 2 tens on the orange side and 3 ones on the yellow side. Ask them to add 14 more sticks: 1 ten to the orange side and 4 ones to the yellow side and determine the sum (3 tens and 7 ones). Let a student volunteer write the corresponding equation (23 + 14 = 37) on the board. Continue with other addition and subtraction equations.

Write 31 + 23 = ? on the board. Have students use their place value mats and craft sticks to solve the equation. Remind students to add the ones first, then the tens. Call on a volunteer to write the sum on the board. Continue with other addition and subtraction equations.

Give students math stories like this to solve: There were 36 ducks in the water. Then 14 ducks flew away. How many ducks were left in the water?

Have students place 36 craft sticks (3 tens and 6 ones) on their mats, then remove 14 sticks (1 ten and 4 ones) and count the number left. Ask a student to write the subtraction equation with the solution on the board. Repeat with other math stories.

Trucking Along with Addition and Subtraction

Make two copies of the "Truck Patterns" page on colored cardstock. Cut out the trucks and label them from 1 to 12. Write a two-digit addition or subtraction equation for students to solve on each truck and laminate the trucks.

Keep the trucks in the math center together with place value mats, craft sticks, rubber bands, and sheets of writing paper. When students have extra time, they can go to the center and choose six or more of the trucks, copy down the equations, and use the manipulatives to find the solutions. You could make the activity self-checking by providing an answer key.

Craft Stick Math

Use a large piece of Styrofoam™ packing or fill a shoe box with dried beans or sand. Write two-digit addition or subtraction equations at the top of jumbo craft sticks and write answers at the bottom. Stand the sticks up in the Styrofoam™, beans, or sand so that the answers cannot be seen. Students copy the equations and write the solutions. To check their answers, they remove the craft sticks.

0-7682-2911-1 *Fast Ideas for Busy Teachers: Math*

Truck Patterns..

0-7682-2911-1 *Fast Ideas for Busy Teachers: Math*

Adding and Subtracting Two-Digit Numbers

Fishbowl Math

Make copies of the "Fish Patterns" on colored paper. Cut out the fish and laminate each shape. On each fish, write a two-digit addition or subtraction equation with a permanent marker. Put the fish in a plastic bowl or small pail.

Each day select five students to "catch" a fish and write the equations on the board. The students with the fish solve the equations at the board while the rest of the students solve them at their desks.

Repeat the activity with other sets of students over a period of days until the fishbowl is empty and all students have had a chance to catch a fish. Reward the class by filling the bowl with fish-shaped crackers to share!

Hands-On

Provide students with many hands-on experiences while learning to add and subtract two-digit numbers. Items in the math center like linking cube "trains," paper clip chains, and craft sticks bundled together with rubber bands make ideal manipulatives for solving two-digit addition and subtraction equations.

Let's Go Fishing

Glue a small piece of strip magnet to the back of each fish and place the fish in a plastic pail in the math center. On a rainy day, let students "go fishing." Attach a paper clip to a piece of string and tie the string to an unsharpened pencil. Students put the hook (paper clip) in the pail. When a student catches a fish, he takes it back to his desk and solves the equation.

Personal Math Stories

Write two numbers on the board, such as 15 and 47. Then say a math story that involves adding the two numbers and uses the name of one of the students. Example: Mia saw 57 yellow parrots at the zoo. She also saw 15 green parrots at the zoo. How many parrots did Mia see in all?

Have students determine the math operation (addition), then write and solve the equation. Next, ask the student named to make up a math story with the same pair of numbers but that uses subtraction to find the answer. She tells her math story to the class and they solve it.

Repeat the activity with other pairs of numbers and other students' names. Alternate between math stories that use addition and ones that require subtraction.

0-7682-2911-1 *Fast Ideas for Busy Teachers: Math*

Fish Patterns..........

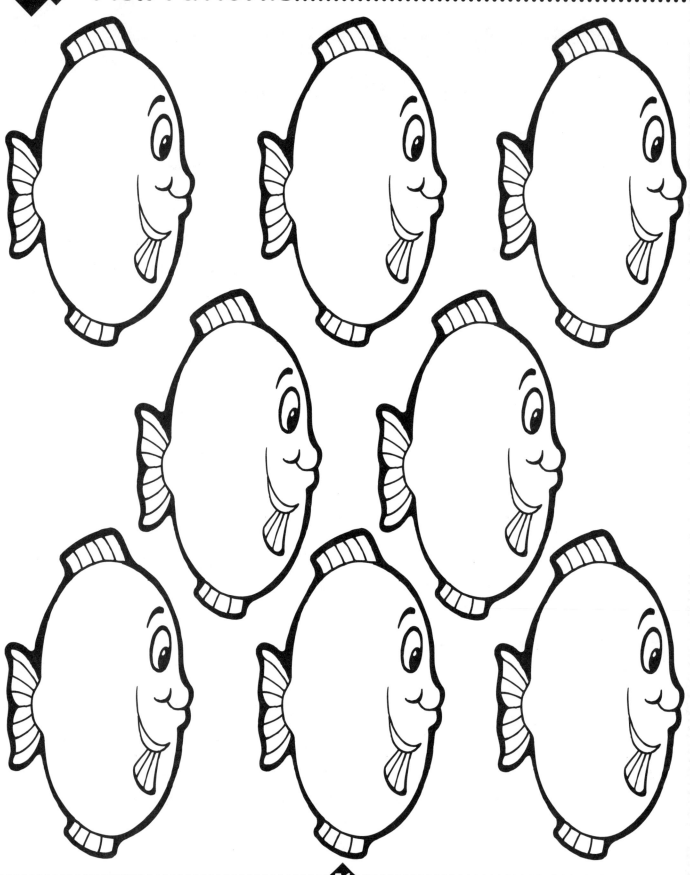

0-7682-2911-1 *Fast Ideas for Busy Teachers: Math*

Counting Coins

Compare the Coins

Have the class compare the sizes, shapes, and colors of real coins. Discuss the different pictures on both sides of each denomination. Remember to point out the difference between "new" quarters and "old" quarters. Talk about how the backs of the new quarters are different and why.

Give each student a set of play coins and ask them to arrange them in order from least to greatest value.

Skip Count with Coins

Help students develop number sense and money sense by having them skip count with coins. Let students use play money or coin sets they made from the "Coin Patterns" page. Guide the class through the following activities:

Count out 10 dimes. Count by tens to a dollar: 10¢, 20¢, 30¢ . . .

Use the same 10 dimes. Take away one dime at a time, counting backwards from a dollar by tens: $1.00, 90¢, 80¢ . . .

Put pennies in stacks of 10. Count the stacks by tens to find the total amount of money.

Count out 20 nickels. Count by fives to a dollar: 5¢, 10¢, 15¢ . . .

Use the same 20 nickels. Take away one nickel at a time, counting backwards from a dollar by fives: $1.00, 95¢, 90¢ . . .

Combination Challenge

Put some play coins in a small paper bag. If students are just beginning to learn to count coins, you may want to use only pennies and nickels in the bag. Call on a student to draw two or three coins from the bag. Have the student name the coins and state the total value. Repeat this activity several times.

Extend the activity by dividing students into pairs and giving each pair a set of coins in a small paper bag. Students can take turns drawing coins from the bag and stating the amount. As students' abilities grow, increase the number and denomination of coins drawn.

Coin Sets

Provide sets of coins for students to manipulate as they explore money concepts. Give each student a copy of "Coin Patterns" reproduced on construction paper or cardstock. Students can color the pennies brown. After they cut out the coins, they can store them in plastic sandwich bags.

0-7682-2911-1 *Fast Ideas for Busy Teachers: Math*

Coin Patterns.........................

© McGraw-Hill Children's Publishing

0-7682-2911-1 *Fast Ideas for Busy Teachers: Math*

Counting and Comparing Coins

Piggy Bank Math

This activity works well with small groups at the math center. Let students use a real piggy bank if one is available. If not, use a plain brown lunch bag and draw a pig's face on it. Place some plastic or paper coins on a table by the bank.

Ask a student to select one coin and put it into the bank. The student names the coin and draws it on a piece of paper before putting the coin in the bank. (To draw the coin, the student can simply draw a circle and write its denomination (1¢, 5¢, etc.) in the circle.

Repeat with other students in the group until four or five coins are in the bank. Students should draw all of the coins on the same piece of paper. Have students tally the drawings to determine the total amount in the bank.

For a follow-up activity, give each student a copy of "Piggy Bank Math" to complete.

Coin Collection

Familiarize students with money by making a display of real coins. Tape two pennies, nickels, dimes, quarters, and half dollars on index cards so that the front and back of each type of coin shows. Label the cards with the word (penny) and the value (1¢). Display the coin cards in the math center.

Money Riddles

Give students a set of play or paper coins. Put two real coins in a change purse without showing them to the class. Then ask them to guess what coins are in the purse by using the clues.

Example: There are two coins in the purse. They add up to 35 cents. What are the coins?

Let students manipulate their coins to find the answer. Ask a volunteer to name the two coins you have in the purse. To check, open the purse and show them the coins. Repeat the activity with other coin combinations.

As a follow-up, divide the class into small groups. Give each group an envelope and a set of plastic or paper coins. Have students in each group take turns putting coins in the envelopes and giving clues as to the number of coins and their value. The other members of the group manipulate their set of play coins to find the answers.

0-7682-2911-1 *Fast Ideas for Busy Teachers: Math*

Piggy Bank Math...................................

Cut out the coins. Glue them on the piggy banks. Use all the coins.

Write how much money is in each bank.

_____ ¢

_____ ¢

_____ ¢

0-7682-2911-1 *Fast Ideas for Busy Teachers: Math*

Finding Equivalent Amounts

Coin Counting Tip

When adding the value of coins, encourage students to begin with the highest denomination first. Then progressively add coins of lesser value.

Coin Equivalents

Divide the class into small groups and give each group a collection of plastic or paper coins: pennies, nickels, dimes, and quarters. Have members of each group manipulate the coins to create different coin combinations worth 5¢, 10¢, 25¢, and 50¢. Challenge them to find several combinations for 10¢, 25¢, and 50¢.

Students could represent 25¢ using 25 pennies; 2 dimes and 1 nickel; 5 nickels; 4 nickels and 5 pennies; 2 dimes and 5 pennies; etc.

Have students draw pictures of their different combinations on a sheet of paper. Combine students' lists to make a class chart.

Why Change a Dollar Bill?

When students use real-life applications of math skills, their math lessons become more meaningful. Ask students to brainstorm for reasons why people would need to exchange a dollar bill for a dollar's worth of coins. (To have coins to make a telephone call, buy a soda from a vending machine, plug a parking meter, or divide the dollar between two people.)

Have students choose one of the ideas suggested during the brainstorming session and draw a picture showing the situation.

Equal Values

Have each student fold a sheet of paper into fourths. Write 30¢ on the board. Ask students to draw coins (circles with 1¢, 5¢, 10¢, 25¢, or 50¢ written on them) in each section of their papers to show four different coin combinations that equal 30¢. They can share their combinations with the class. List their ideas on a sheet of chart paper. The class will be amazed at the variety of ways they can make 30¢. Repeat the activity with another amount.

Equivalent Sets

Divide the class into small groups and give each group a large sheet of drawing paper. Assign each group an amount between 35¢ and 90¢. Have each group write that amount at the top of the page, then work together to make a chart showing at least four coin combinations for the designated amount. Students can draw the coins (circles with the amounts written inside) on their paper or they can cut out paper coins using the "Coin Patterns" and glue them on their charts.

0-7682-2911-1 *Fast Ideas for Busy Teachers: Math*

 # Finding Equivalent Amounts

A Money Mobile

Creating money mobiles is a fun project for students to show equivalent amounts. Make a copy of the "Money Mobile" patterns on cardstock or construction paper for each student. Students write their names and an amount such as 45¢ on the designated circle. Have students cut out coins and glue them onto the remaining circles to show four different combinations equal to that amount. Use a hole punch to make holes where indicated on the circles. Finally, connect the circles together with yarn and hang.

Fill Your Plates

Divide students into pairs and give each pair a set of paper or plastic coins and two paper plates. One student places some coins in her plate. The other student determines the amount and puts a different set of coins of equivalent value on his plate. After both partners confirm that the sets of coins are equivalent, they switch roles.

Coin Concentration

Make copies of the "Coin Concentration Cards" on cardstock. You will need half as many copies as you have students. Divide the class into pairs and give each pair a set of cards. Have students cut out the cards. Explain how to play "Coin Concentration":

Shuffle the cards. Place them facedown in rows on the table or floor.

Take turns turning over two cards at a time. If the coins on the cards show the same value, keep the cards. If they are not equal amounts, return them facedown to their original places.

Continue until all pairs are matched. The player with the most cards wins.

Extension:

Have students make additional cards for a more challenging game. Give them blank cards, the same size as the Concentration Coin cards and a copy of the Coin Patterns page. Have students cut out the coins and glue them onto the blank cards to make equivalent pairs. Add their cards to the original set and play again.

0-7682-2911-1 *Fast Ideas for Busy Teachers: Math*

A Money Mobile

Finding Equivalent Amounts

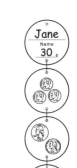

Write your name and an amount on the first circle.

On the other circles, show other ways to equal that amount.

Cut out the circles.

Punch holes.

Tie the circles together with yarn.

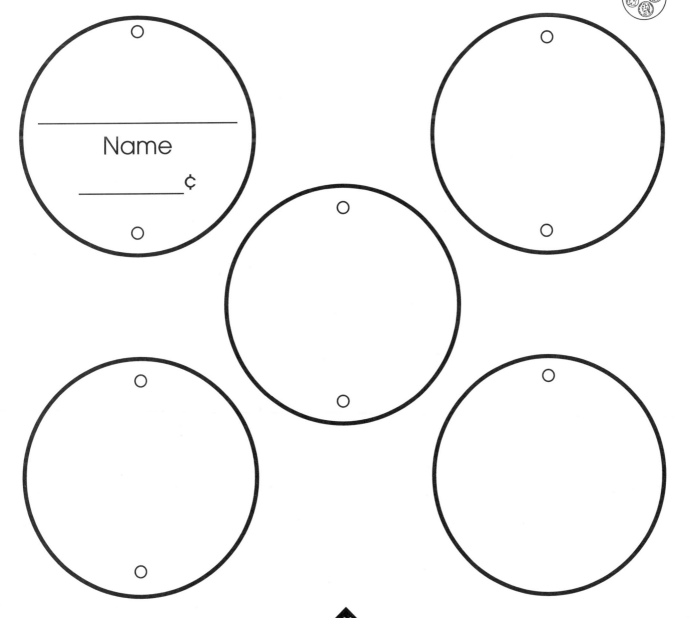

Name

© McGraw-Hill Children's Publishing

0-7682-2911-1 *Fast Ideas for Busy Teachers: Math*

Concentration Coin Cards ....

0-7682-2911-1 *Fast Ideas for Busy Teachers: Math*

Making Purchases

Exact Change Needed

Gather several items, such as school supplies or toys, and attach price tags to them. Display the items at the front of the room. Give each student a set of paper or plastic coins. Hold up items one at a time and state the prices. Have students place on their desks the appropriate coins (exact amount) needed to buy the items.

Toys for Sale

Give each student a copy of "Toys for Sale." When they finish work, pair up students and have partners compare their answers with each other.

Can You Buy It?

Make copies of the two pages of the "Can You Buy It?" cards. Pair up students and give each pair the two sets of cards to cut apart. Tell students to keep the money cards and item cards separate.

To play, shuffle both sets of cards and place facedown in two piles.

Students take turns picking one card from each pile.

> If they have enough money on the card to buy the item, they return the money card to the bottom of its pile and keep the item card.

> If they do not have enough money, they return both cards to the bottom of the piles.

Players shuffle and replay cards as needed. Continue until players have "bought" all of the item cards.

A Classroom Store

Gather small, nonvaluable toys, manipulatives, and objects like pens, pencils, pages of stickers, etc. Small, clean empty containers taped shut, such as half-pint milk cartons, sample-size toothpaste boxes, or travel-size shampoo bottles work well, also.

Put price stickers on the items and store in a shoe box in the math center together with a collection of plastic or paper coins. Students can use the items to set up a store where they practice making purchases. Using real objects adds interest when students work with money. They can take turns being the clerk and customers, "buying" items with play coins, and making change for purchases.

0-7682-2911-1 *Fast Ideas for Busy Teachers: Math*

Toys for Sale..

Which coins do you need to buy the toys?

Draw them in the boxes.

Can You Buy It? Item Cards......................

0-7682-2911-1 *Fast Ideas for Busy Teachers: Math*

Can You Buy It? Money Cards...................

0-7682-2911-1 *Fast Ideas for Busy Teachers: Math*

Graphing

"Classy" Graphs

Take a picture of your class, enlarge it, and display it on a bulletin board or computer monitor. Let students use the picture to answer questions like the ones listed.

How many boys are in the picture?

How many girls are in the picture?

How many students have blond hair?

How many students are wearing red?

How many students are wearing glasses?

How many students are wearing short-sleeved shirts?

Record the answers on the board. Make a bar graph on chart paper. Have students help fill in the categories and color the bars to illustrate the information.

Reusable Graphs

Make graphs for the math center that students can use over and over again. Draw a blank grid on white paper and laminate it. When using the graph, students can write the title and categories in grease pencil and use self-sticking notes or small squares of paper and a glue stick to add data to the graph. The graphs can be easily wiped clean and reused.

Concrete Graphs

Concrete materials and hands-on experiences give students a firm grasp of mathematical concepts. To introduce students to graphing, have them make graphs using real objects. Divide students into small groups. Give each group a large grid drawn on chart paper and 25 to 50 small items of different shapes or colors, such as paper clips, game chips, or buttons. Have students sort the items by color, size, or shape, then glue or tape them to the grid to form a bar graph. Students then count and record how many there are of each item. Concrete graphs are a great way to prepare students for working with diagrams and graphs that are more abstract.

Edible Graphs

Students can use small candies that come in different colors, several shapes of pretzels, or animal crackers for a tasty graphing activity. Divide the class into small groups and give each group a bag of edible items to graph.

Before students count the items, have them guess how many they have of each color or shape and write down their predictions. Students then sort, count, and graph the results to see how close their predictions were. You can combine the results and make a large class graph on chart paper. After they finish, let students in each group divide the treats among themselves for a tasty snack.

0-7682-2911-1 *Fast Ideas for Busy Teachers: Math*

Graphing

Sticker Graphs

Divide the class into small groups. Give each group a bag containing 20 to 30 stickers. Each bag should have five kinds of stickers with a similar theme. (One bag could have five kinds of animals; another could have five different colored star stickers or five different flowers.)

Tell the groups to sort their stickers to find out how many there are of each kind and record the information on scrap paper. Then give each student a copy of "A Sticker Graph." Provide extra stickers for each group, if needed, and have each student do the following:

1. Take one sample of each type of sticker in the bag.

2. Place these stickers along the bottom of the graph.

3. Color the graph to show how many you had of each kind of sticker.

Afterwards, have groups share their graphs with the class.

Reusable Graphs

Paint or draw a blank graph on a small light-colored chalkboard using permanent paint or marker. Students can write the title and data on the graph in chalk and erase it when they finish the graph.

Life-Size Graphs

Students can make a life-size graph by placing themselves on the grid! Use masking tape to mark off a large grid on the classroom, hall, or gym floor. If the weather is suitable, you could take this activity outside and make the grid with chalk on the playground.

Label the grid with numbers along the left side. Along the bottom, place various pictures or items belonging to one category. You could use pictures or pieces of different types of fruit, cans containing different types of soup or vegetables, equipment representing different sports, etc.

Ask students to line up in rows behind the picture of the item they like the best. Have the class help you count how many students are in each row and record the information on the board. Discuss the results with questions like these:

Which fruit did most students like best?

Which type of soup was the least favorite?

Did more students prefer baseball or soccer?

How many students chose peas and carrots?

Change the pictures or items and have students rearrange themselves to make a new graph.

0-7682-2911-1 *Fast Ideas for Busy Teachers: Math*

A Sticker Graph ....

Number of Stickers

6

5

4

3

2

1

0

Glue Sticker Here	Glue Sticker Here	Glue Sticker Here	Glue Sticker Here	Glue Sticker Here

0-7682-2911-1 *Fast Ideas for Busy Teachers: Math*

Measuring with Nonstandard Units

Step by Step

Have students use their feet to measure the length of the room or the width of the hallway by walking "heel to toe" and counting steps. Afterwards, let them compare their results with one another. Discuss why the number varies from child to child. (Since foot sizes vary, students with longer feet would need fewer foot-lengths to span the length of the room or the width of the hallway.) Ask them to estimate how far the distance would be in your "foot-lengths." Measure and compare the results to their estimates.

Tell the class that long ago a man's foot was used to measure length. Explain that sometimes measurements differed because men's foot sizes differed. Eventually, people decided to use standard units to keep measurements consistent.

A good way to demonstrate would be to use two pairs of men's shoes, one about a size 8 and the other about a size 12. Have students measure the same length using the two different pairs of shoes. How much difference did they find? Why would it be a problem if everyone measured distance using different sized units?

String Measurement

Give each student a piece of string to use as a nonstandard unit of measurement. Strings could be about 10 to 20 inches long, but not exactly the same length. Tell students to measure objects with their strings and find one that is shorter than their string. Have them draw the object on a piece of paper and label the drawing "Shorter Than My String."

Next, have students measure objects to find one that is longer than their string, draw it on another sheet of paper, and label that drawing "Longer Than My String."

Show students a variety of objects and ask them to guess if each one is longer or shorter than their strings. Have them write the name of each object and the word "longer" or "shorter." They can check their predictions by measuring the objects with their string.

Many Ways to Measure

Introduce students to the concept of measuring length by letting them first use nonstandard units of measure. Keep a supply of nonstandard measuring units in the math center. Paper clips, plastic links, toothpicks, cotton swabs, pencils, and craft sticks all work well as "measuring sticks" for finding the length of objects.

Students can create their own nonstandard units by cutting a strip of paper to a desired length. Have students invent fun names for their units such as "wibble" or "gorp." They can use their units at home or school and report how long items are in wibbles or gorps.

0-7682-2911-1 *Fast Ideas for Busy Teachers: Math*

Measuring with Nonstandard Units

The Mysterious Broom

Hold up a broom and say, "I have a strange broom here. Do you know why it's so strange? Every time I try to measure the handle, I come up with a different length. Do you think my broom is growing and shrinking?"

Ask students to help measure your broom handle. Give one student a very short pencil and ask her to measure by placing the pencil end to end along the handle. Record the measurement on the board.

Tell students you want to double-check and have another student measure the handle, but this time give the student a longer pencil. Record the second measurement next to the first one.

Tell students, "See, I told you it was a mysterious broom. Let's try it one more time." Ask a third student to measure using a new unsharpened pencil. Record the third measurement.

Discuss why the three measurements differed. Did the broom handle get longer or shorter? Have students brainstorm for objects with a consistent length they could use to make measurements, such as paper clips, toothpicks, or chalkboard erasers.

All About Measuring

Read *Super Sand Castle Saturday* by Stuart J. Murphy aloud to the class. This story about three children and a sand castle-building contest reinforces the differences between standard and nonstandard measuring units.

Keep a copy of this book in the math center for students to enjoy when they have free time.

How Long?

Give each student a copy of the activity "How Long?" and a nonstandard unit for measuring, such as a cotton swab or paper clip. Students should draw and label the unit they use at the top of the page. Have each student select six items in the classroom to measure and record the results.

They can list the items either by drawing pictures of them or by writing the names of the objects.

Measuring Chains

Give pairs of students 30–40 paper clips. Show the class how to attach the paper clips to form chains. Hand out copies of "A Measuring Chain." Tell students to use their chains to measure the items listed on the page. Before measuring, have students estimate the length of each object and record their guesses on the paper. Then have them check their estimates by measuring.

 0-7682-2911-1 *Fast Ideas for Busy Teachers: Math*

 **How Long?**..

My unit of measure

What I measured	Number of units
1.	
2.	
3.	

What I measured	Number of units
4.	
5.	
6.	

0-7682-2911-1 *Fast Ideas for Busy Teachers: Math*

A Measuring Chain.....................................

Guess the length of each item.
Write your guess on the chart.
Make a chain of paper clips.
Measure the items to check your guess.

	Our guess	Our measurement
1. How long is a chalkboard eraser?	_____ paper clips	_____ paper clips
2. How long is your pencil?	_____ paper clips	_____ paper clips
3. How wide is the doorway?	_____ paper clips	_____ paper clips
4. How wide is your desk?	_____ paper clips	_____ paper clips
5. How tall is your chair?	_____ paper clips	_____ paper clips

0-7682-2911-1 *Fast Ideas for Busy Teachers: Math*

Measuring with Standard Units

It's in the Bag!

Decorate a large paper bag and label it "It's in the Bag." Fill the bag with paintbrushes, zippers, keys, key chains, pieces of ribbon, and other small objects that can easily be measured in centimeters or inches. You will need at least one item per student. Shake the bag and have each student reach in and select an object.

Show students how to line up their rulers carefully with the item they are measuring so that they get accurate measurements. Students measure the objects and record the measurements on the board or a sheet of chart paper.

Toy Line-Up

Invite students to bring their stuffed toys to school. Attach a yardstick or tape measure securely to the wall. Have students measure the toys and record the measurements on a chart. When they finish, have the class arrange the toys in order according to height.

For a fun follow-up, give each student a copy of "Check These Stripes!" Have students use a centimeter ruler to measure the stripes on each toy animal.

Answers to "Check These Stripes!" 1. 2 cm, 2. 4 cm, 3. 5 cm, 4. 3 cm, 5. 3 cm, 6. 4 cm, 7. 5 cm, 8. 2 cm

All Kinds of Lengths

Ask each student to bring an interesting object to class that is between 4 and 12 inches long. Have students draw a picture of their objects, measure them, and record their lengths. Post the pictures on one section of the bulletin board with the title "Between 4 and 12 Inches."

On another day, have students bring objects that are less than four inches and repeat the procedure described above. Label the second section "Less Than 4 Inches."

Finally, have students bring objects that are greater than 12 inches long. Label the section for these objects "More Than 12 Inches." Provide yardsticks, folding rulers, tape measures, and tailor's tapes to help students measure the lengths of their super-sized finds.

Measuring Length and Weight

Henry Pluckrose encourages readers to participate in measurement activities through vibrantly colored photographs of familiar objects, informative text, and related questions. His two books, *Length* and *Weight* would make great additions to the math center.

0-7682-2911-1 *Fast Ideas for Busy Teachers: Math*

Name _____ Date _____

Check These Stripes! ....

Use a centimeter ruler.
Measure the stripes.
Write your answers on the lines.

A. _____ cm

B. _____ cm

C. _____ cm

D. _____ cm

E. _____ cm

F. _____ cm

G. _____ cm

H. _____ cm

0-7682-2911-1 *Fast Ideas for Busy Teachers: Math*

Measuring and Comparing Weight

Mystery Objects

Ask each student to bring an object to class in a paper grocery bag. Staple the bags close when they arrive so the objects remain secret. Ask each student to give one clue about the object and pass the bag around the class. Let students use the clue and the weight of the object to determine what might be in the bag. Give each student a list on lined paper that includes all the names of their classmates. Have them write what they think is in each bag next to the classmate's name.

After all students have shared their objects, display the objects in the room.

Challenge students to select three or four of the objects and arrange them in order from lightest to heaviest. Check using a small scale.

In Balance

Measuring in first grade should include using a balance scale to compare weights. Keep plenty of small items with the scale in the math center. Students can estimate how many plastic bears (or other counters) it will take to balance another object. Let students search for other small objects in the room to weigh and compare.

More or Less Than a Pound?

Hold up a one-pound bag of sugar or can of vegetables and point to the weight on the label. Pass the item around so everyone has a chance to experience how much one pound weighs. Without using a scale, ask students to find something in the class that weighs more than a pound and something that weighs less. Set the items that weigh less on one side and the items that weigh more on the other side.

Have students explain how they determined the weights. Follow up by giving each student a copy of the activity "More or Less than a Pound?" and have students complete the activity at home.

More or Less?

Set up a weigh station in the math center. When time permits, have students go to the center individually or in small groups. Provide two items for each student to weigh. Tape an index card to each item. Items that work well are boxes of crayons or colored pencils, a travel clock, hairbrush, calculator, small notebooks, and fresh fruit.

Tell students their task is to weigh two items, record the weights on the attached cards, and find something in the room that weighs more and something that weighs less than that item. They can write the names or draw pictures of the items they weigh on the backs of the index cards.

 0-7682-2911-1 *Fast Ideas for Busy Teachers: Math*

Name _____ Date _____

 # More or Less Than a Pound?.......................

Look in your kitchen for foods that come in packages.
Read the weight on the label.

1. Find a food item that weighs one pound.

   Draw it and label the picture.

2. Find one food item that you think weighs more than
   one pound.

   Draw it and label the picture.

   Check the label. How much does it weigh? _____

   Did you guess correctly? _____

0-7682-2911-1 *Fast Ideas for Busy Teachers: Math*

Probability

A Button Game

Show students three red buttons and one white button as you put them into a bag. Shake the bag and ask students to guess which color you will pick. Without looking in the bag, pick a button and show it to the class. Record its color on the board. Put the button back in the bag.

Ask the class to predict which color they think someone would pick if he selected a button without looking five times in a row. Ask four students to each select a button without looking, record its color, and return the button to the bag.

Discuss the results. Guide the class into seeing that since there were more red buttons than white ones, it was more likely that someone would choose a red one more often than a white one.

A Color Game

Pair up students and give each pair a paper bag and a copy of "A Color Game." Provide enough buttons or colored game markers for the class to play the game. Each pair should select two different-colored buttons or game markers and color the A and B circles to indicate their chosen colors.

Explain to students that they will be playing three games with a different number of buttons each time. For each game, they will select a button from the bag, record its color, and return the button to the bag. They will do this five times per game.

To record the color chosen each time, students color the appropriate squares on their sheets. When everyone finishes, display the finished pages to share the results with the class.

A Shape Game

Make copies of "A Shape Game" on cardstock and give each pair of students a copy. Students should cut out the shape cards and the chart. Students put the shape cards in a paper bag and take turns shaking the bag and taking a card without looking. They should make a tally mark on the chart indicating the shape chosen. Remind them to return the shape card to the bag each time.

Have students repeat the procedure ten times. Afterwards, they count their tally marks and write the number to show how many times they chose each shape. They should color the shape they chose most often. Discuss the results with the class.

© McGraw-Hill Children's Publishing

0-7682-2911-1 *Fast Ideas for Busy Teachers: Math*

 # A Color Game...

Color the circles to match your buttons.

Each time you pick a button from your bag, color a square to show what color you chose.

Game 1 Use 4 A and 1 B. Pick a button five times.

A

B

How many times did you pick A? ____ B? ____

Game 2 Use 4 A and 10 B. Pick a button five times.

A

B

How many times did you pick A? ____ B? ____

Game 3 Use 4 A and 4 B. Pick a button five times.

A

B

How many times did you pick A? ____ B? ____

0-7682-2911-1 *Fast Ideas for Busy Teachers: Math*

A Shape Game...

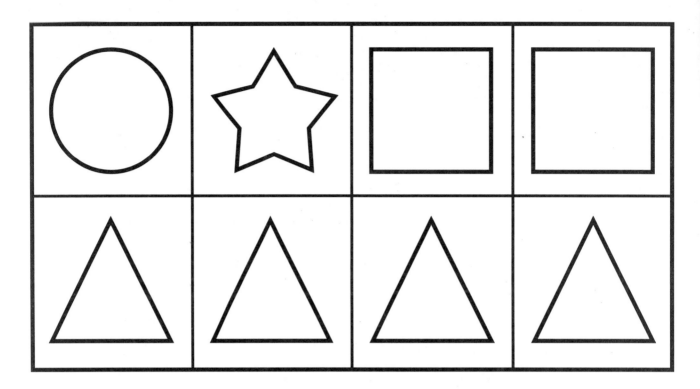

Number of Times Picked

○			
☆			
□			
△			

0-7682-2911-1 *Fast Ideas for Busy Teachers: Math*